The Perfect End Time Plan

The Church's Greatest Hour

by

Joshua Alvarez

The Perfect End Time Plan

The Church's Greatest Hour

by

Joshua Alvarez

Publishing Company

Joshua Alvarez

First Edition

Copyright © 2016

ISBN-13: 978-0997308501 (JOSHUA ALVAREZ)

ISBN-10: 0997308508

Unless otherwise noted, all Scripture quotations are from the New American Standard Version of the Bible.

Scripture quotations taken from the New American Standard Bible®, Copyright © 1960, 1962, 1963, 1968, 1971, 1972, 1973, 1975, 1977, 1995 by The Lockman Foundation. Used by permission. (www.Lockman.org)

Scripture quotations taken from the Holy Bible, New King James Version®. Copyright © 1982 by Thomas Nelson, Inc. All rights reserved.

To my beautiful wife Alyssa, and my lovely daughter Purity I love you both so dearly. Lastly, to my precious Lord and Savior Jesus Christ, to whom I owe everything.

Abomination of Desolation

"In the middle of the week he will put a stop to sacrifice and grain offering; and on the wing of abominations *will come* one who makes desolate, even until a complete destruction, one that is decreed, is poured out on the one who makes desolate." **Daniel 9:27**

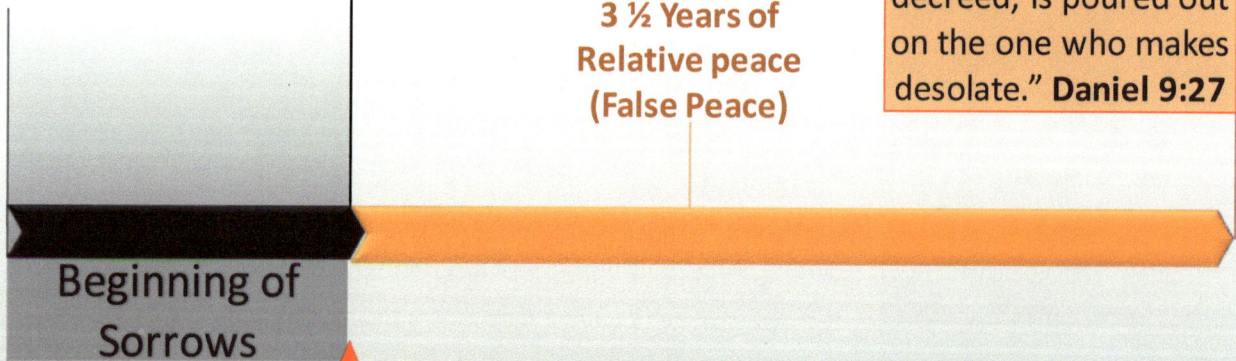

"Then I saw when the Lamb broke one of the seven seals...Behold, a white horse, and he who sat on it had a bow; and a crown was given to him, and he went out conquering and to conquer." **Revelation 6:2**

1ST Seal: Antichrist

3 ½ Years of Relative peace (False Peace)

Beginning of Sorrows

Seven Year Covenant with Israel Confirmed

"The prince...he will make a firm covenant with the many for one week" **Daniel 9:26,27**

SEVEN YEAR COVENANT

3 ½ Years Great Tribulation

Second Coming of Christ

"Then I saw when the Lamb broke one of the seven seals"
Revelation 6:1

**Abomination
of
Desolation**

"Then I saw when the Lamb broke one of the seven seals...Behold, a white horse, and he who sat on it had a bow; and a crown was given to him, and he went out conquering and to conquer." **Revelation 6:2**

"In the middle of the week he will put a stop to sacrifice and grain offering; and on the wing of abominations *will come* one who makes desolate, even until a complete destruction, one that is decreed, is poured out on the one who makes desolate." **Daniel 9:27**

1ST Seal: Antichrist

Emergence of Antichrist

3 ½ Years of Relative peace (False Peace)

Beginning of Sorrows

Seven Year Covenant with Israel Confirmed

"The prince...he will make a firm covenant with the many for one week"
Daniel 9:26,27

3 ½ Years Great Tribulation

EMERGENCE OF THE ANTICHRIST (FALSE SAVIOR)

THE BEGINNING OF SORROWS:
Matthew 24:4-8
- False Christ
- Wars and Rumors of Wars
- Nation will Rise Against Nation (Race against race)
- Kingdom Against Kingdom
- Famines
- Earthquakes

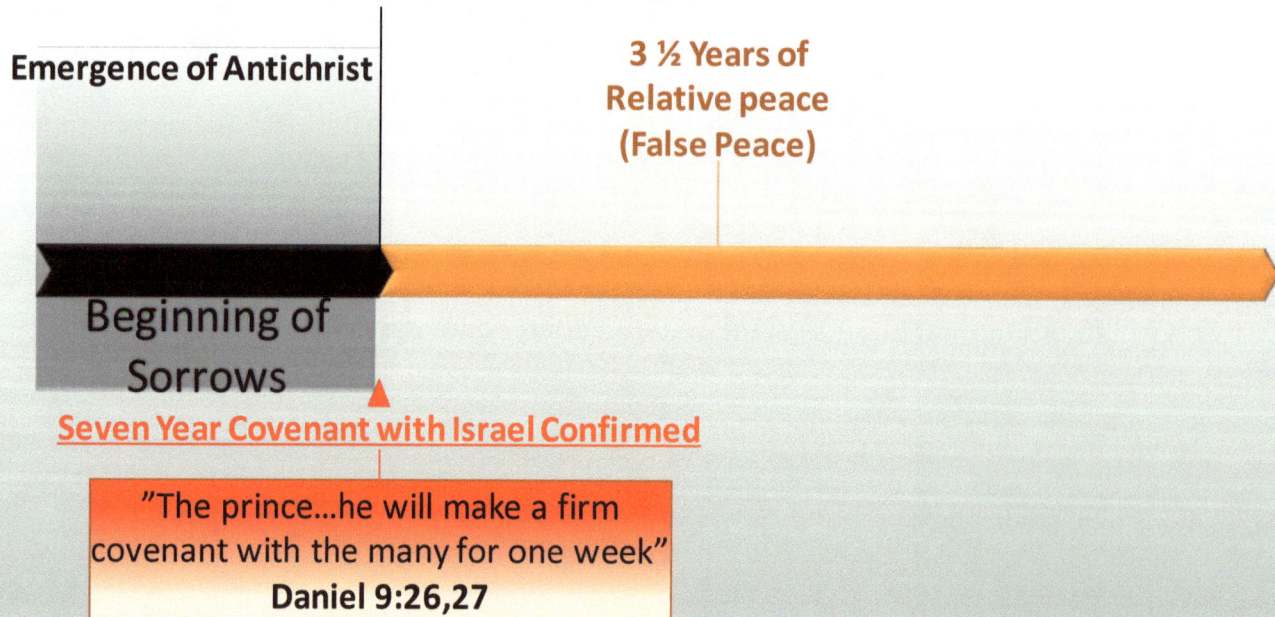

Emergence of Antichrist

3 ½ Years of Relative peace (False Peace)

Beginning of Sorrows

Seven Year Covenant with Israel Confirmed

"The prince...he will make a firm covenant with the many for one week"
Daniel 9:26,27

FALSE PEACE:

- "Behold, a white horse, and he who sat on it had a bow; and a crown was given to him, and he went out conquering and to conquer." **Revelation 6:2** (Bow without arrows)
- "The prince...he will make a firm covenant with the many for one week" **Daniel 9:26,27**
- "While they are saying, 'Peace and safety!' then destruction will come upon them suddenly like labor pains upon a woman with child, and they will not escape." **1 Thessalonians 5:3**

3 ½ Years Great Tribulation

Second Coming of Christ

"In the middle of the week he will put a stop to sacrifice and grain offering; and on the wing of abominations *will come* one who makes desolate, even until a complete destruction, one that is decreed, is poured out on the one who makes desolate." **Daniel 9:27**

Antichrist Emerges

"Small horn that grows exceedingly Great" – Daniel 8:9

The Setting:

Birth Pangs – Matthew 24:5-8

☐ False Christ

☐ Wars

☐ Nation against Nation (Ethnos-Race)

☐ Kingdom against Kingdom (Economy)

☐ Famines

☐ Earthquakes (Shakings, Commotions)

"But all these things are merely the beginning of birth pangs" – Matthew 24:8

"And he will make a firm covenant with the many for one week, but in the middle of the week he will put a stop to sacrifice and grain offering; and on the wing of abominations will come one who makes desolate, even complete destruction, one that is decreed, is poured out on the one who makes desolate." Daniel 9:27

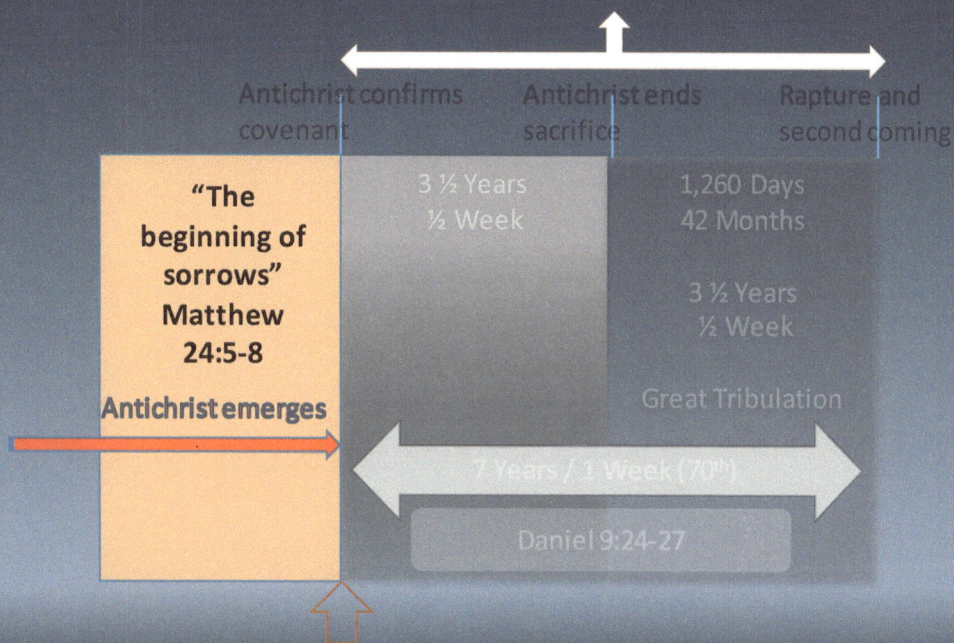

Antichrist confirms covenant

Antichrist ends sacrifice

Rapture and second coming

"The beginning of sorrows" Matthew 24:5-8

Antichrist emerges

3 ½ Years
½ Week

1,260 Days
42 Months

3 ½ Years
½ Week

Great Tribulation

7 Years / 1 Week (70th)

Daniel 9:24-27

"For you your selves know full well that the day of the Lord will come just like a thief in the night. While they are saying, "Peace and safety!" then destruction will come upon them suddenly like labor pains upon a woman with child, and they will not escape." 1 Thessalonians 5:2-3

- "Therefore when you see the ABOMINATION OF DESOLATION which was spoken of through Daniel the prophet, standing in the holy place (let the reader understand)...For then there will be a great tribulation, such as has not occurred since the beginning of the world until now, nor ever will." **Matthew 24:15, 21**

- "But when you see the ABOMINATION OF DESOLATION standing where it should not be (let the reader understand)...For those days will be a time of tribulation such as has not occurred since the beginning of the creation which God created until now, and never will." **Mark 13:14, 19**

- "That you not be quickly shaken from your composure or be disturbed either by a spirit or a message or a letter as if from us, to the effect that the day of the Lord has come. Let no one in any way deceive you, for it will not come unless the apostasy comes first, and the man of lawlessness is revealed, the son of destruction, who opposes and exalts himself above every so-called god or object of worship, so that he takes his seat in the temple of God, displaying himself as being God. " **2 Thessalonians 2:2-4**

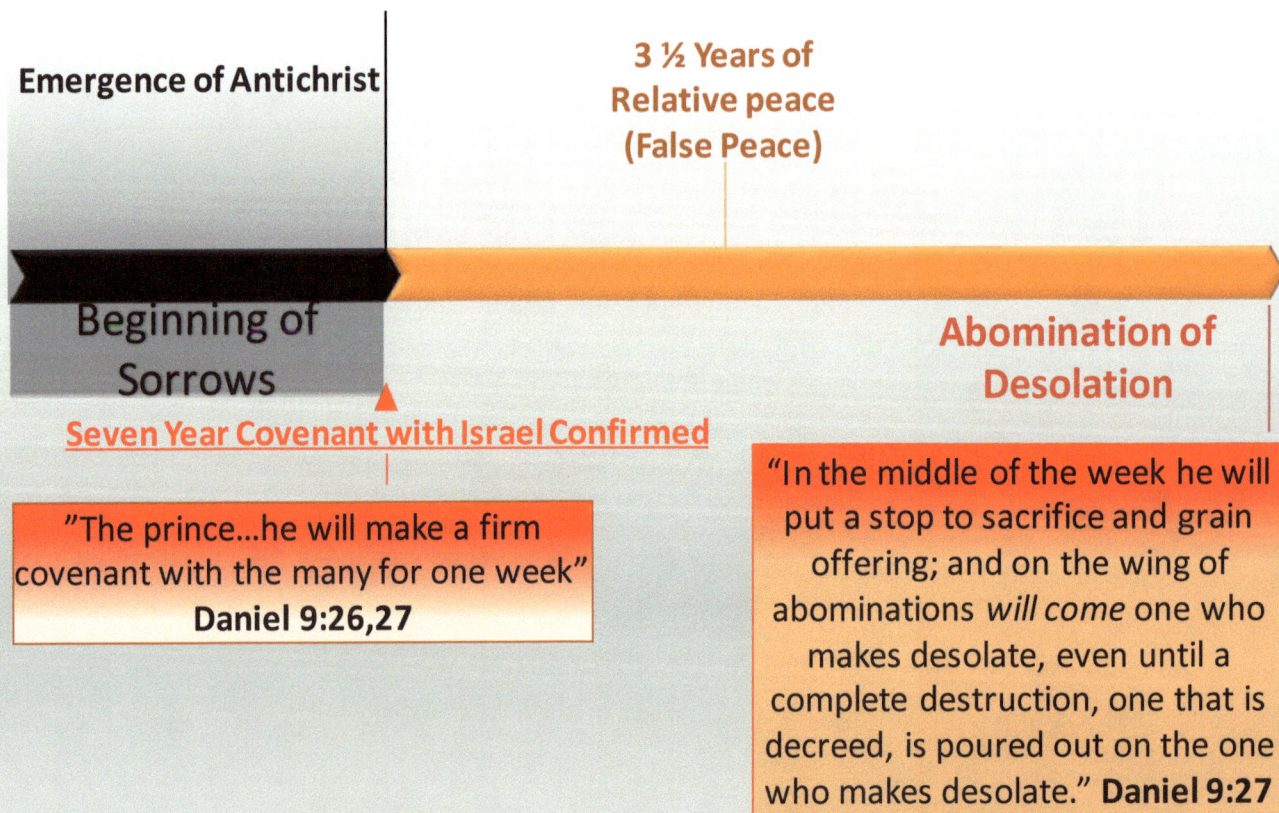

Emergence of Antichrist

3 ½ Years of Relative peace (False Peace)

Beginning of Sorrows

Abomination of Desolation

Seven Year Covenant with Israel Confirmed

"The prince...he will make a firm covenant with the many for one week" **Daniel 9:26,27**

"In the middle of the week he will put a stop to sacrifice and grain offering; and on the wing of abominations *will come* one who makes desolate, even until a complete destruction, one that is decreed, is poured out on the one who makes desolate." **Daniel 9:27**

**3 ½ Years Great
Tribulation**

- "It even magnified *itself* to be equal with the Commander of the host; and it removed the regular sacrifice from Him, and the place of His sanctuary was thrown down. And on account of transgression the host will be given over *to the horn* along with the regular sacrifice; and it will fling truth to the ground and perform *its will* and prosper." **Daniel 8:11-12**
- "Then I heard a holy one speaking, and another holy one said to that particular one who was speaking, 'How long will the vision about the regular sacrifice apply, while the transgression causes horror, so as to allow both the holy place and the host to be trampled?'" **Daniel 8:13**
- "Forces from him will arise, desecrate the sanctuary fortress, and do away with the regular sacrifice. And they will set up the abomination of desolation." **Daniel 11:31**
- "From the time that the regular sacrifice is abolished and the abomination of desolation is set up, there will be 1,290 days." **Daniel 12:11**
- "Then there was given me a measuring rod like a staff; and someone said, 'Get up and measure the temple of God and the altar, and those who worship in it. Leave out the court which is outside the temple and do not measure it, for it has been given to the nations; and they will tread under foot the holy city for forty-two months.'" **Revelation 11:1-2**

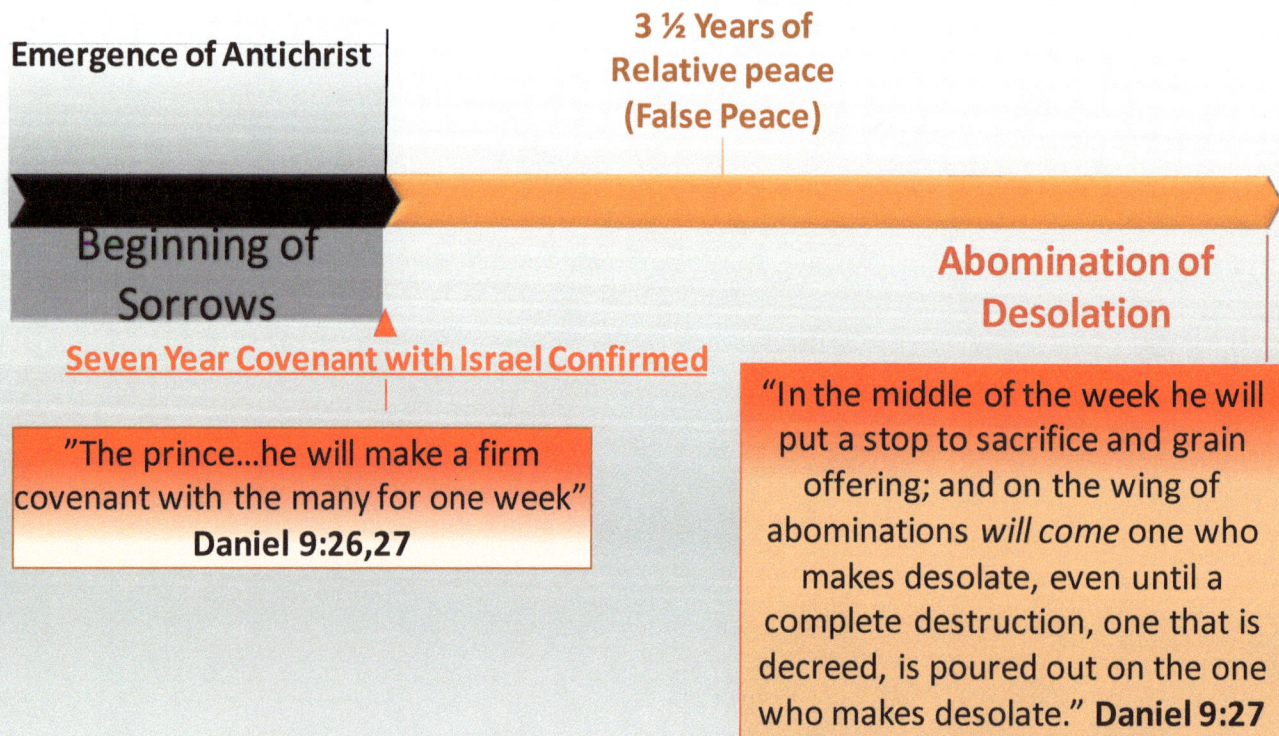

Emergence of Antichrist

3 ½ Years of Relative peace (False Peace)

Beginning of Sorrows

Seven Year Covenant with Israel Confirmed

"The prince...he will make a firm covenant with the many for one week" **Daniel 9:26,27**

Abomination of Desolation

"In the middle of the week he will put a stop to sacrifice and grain offering; and on the wing of abominations *will come* one who makes desolate, even until a complete destruction, one that is decreed, is poured out on the one who makes desolate." **Daniel 9:27**

**3 ½ Years Great
Tribulation**

ABOMINATION OF DESOLATION: THE INVASION OF ISRAEL

- "But when you see Jerusalem surrounded by armies, then recognize that her desolation is near." **Luke 21:20**
- "For the days will come upon you when your enemies will throw up a barricade against you, and surround you and hem you in on every side," **Luke 19:43**
- "For I will gather all the nations against Jerusalem to battle, and the city will be captured, the houses plundered, the women ravished and half of the city exiled, but the rest of the people will not be cut off from the city." **Zechariah 14:2**
- "And they will fall by the edge of the sword, and will be led captive into all the nations; and Jerusalem will be trampled under foot by the Gentiles until the times of the Gentiles are fulfilled." **Luke 21:24**
- "Leave out the court which is outside the temple and do not measure it, for it has been given to the nations; and they will tread under foot the holy city for forty-two months." **Revelation 11:2**
- "Then I heard a holy one speaking, and another holy one said to that particular one who was speaking, "How long will the vision about the regular sacrifice apply, while the transgression causes horror, so as to allow both the holy place and the host to be trampled?" **Daniel 8:13**

The church's calling to stand with Israel:

- "And whoever in the name of a disciple gives to one of these little ones even a cup of cold water to drink, truly I say to you, he shall not lose his reward." **Matthew 10:42**
- "And I will bless those who bless you, And the one who curses you I will curse. And in you all the families of the earth will be blessed." **Genesis 12:3**

END TIME HARVEST:
"But when the crop permits (is ripe), he immediately puts in the sickle, because the harvest has come."
Mark 4:29

"So you will again distinguish between the righteous and the wicked, between one who serves God and one who does not serve Him." **Malachi 3:18**

"Now when they fall they will be granted a little help, and many will join with them in hypocrisy. "Some of those who have insight will fall, in order to refine, purge and make them pure until the end time; because *it is* still *to come* at the appointed time." **Daniel 11:34-35**

Great Revival:
- "The Spirit of the Lord GOD is upon me, Because the LORD has anointed me To bring good news to the afflicted; He has sent me to bind up the brokenhearted, To proclaim liberty to captives And freedom to prisoners; To proclaim the favorable year of the LORD And the day of vengeance of our God...For as the earth brings forth its sprouts, And as a garden causes the things sown in it to spring up, So the Lord GOD will cause righteousness and praise To spring up before all the nations." **Isaiah 61:1-2, 11**
- "AND IT SHALL BE IN THE LAST DAYS,' God says, 'THAT I WILL POUR FORTH OF MY SPIRIT ON ALL MANKIND; AND YOUR SONS AND YOUR DAUGHTERS SHALL PROPHECY, AND YOUR YOUNG MEN SHALL SEE VISIONS, AND YOUR OLD MEN SHALL DREAM DREAMS." **Acts 2:17**

Great Apostasy:
- "Let no one in any way deceive you, for it will not come unless the apostasy comes first, and the man of lawlessness is revealed, the son of destruction," **2 Thessalonians 2:3**
- "Because lawlessness is increased, most people's love will grow cold." **Matthew 24:12**
- "For the time will come when they will not endure sound doctrine; but wanting to have their ears tickled, they will accumulate for themselves teachers in accordance to their own desires," **2 Timothy 4:3**
- "In the latter period of their rule, When the transgressors have run their course (transgression full), A king will arise, Insolent and skilled in intrigue." **Daniel 8:23**

"Then I saw when the Lamb broke one of the seven seals" Revelation 6:1

"When He broke the second seal...a red horse, went out; and to him who sat on it, it was granted to take peace from the earth, and that *men* would slay one another; and a great sword was given to him." **Revelation 6:3,4**

THE GREAT TRIBULATION

"For then there will be a great tribulation, such as has not occurred since the beginning of the world until now, nor ever will." **Matthew 24:21**

2nd Seal:
War

3 ½ Years
Great
Tribulation

3 ½ YEARS GREAT TRIBULATION

The Abomination of Desolation

"The prince...in the middle of the week he will put a stop to sacrifice and grain offering; and on the wing of abominations *will come* one who makes desolate, even until a complete destruction, one that is decreed, is poured out on the one who makes desolate." **Daniel 9:26, 27**

THE GREAT TRIBULATION 3 ½ YEARS

"Therefore when you see the ABOMINATION OF DESOLATION which was spoken of through Daniel the prophet, standing in the holy place (let the reader understand), then those who are in Judea must flee to the mountains. Whoever is on the housetop must not go down to get the things out that are in his house. Whoever is in the field must not turn back to get his cloak. But woe to those who are pregnant and to those who are nursing babies in those days!.. For then there will be a great tribulation, such as has not occurred since the beginning of the world until now, nor ever will." **Matthew 24:15-21**

The Abomination of Desolation

3 ½ YEAR GREAT TRIBULATION:

- "He will speak out against the Most High and wear down the saints of the Highest One, and he will intend to make alterations in times and in law; and they will be given into his hand for a time, times, and half a time (3 ½ years)." **Daniel 7:25**
- "Leave out the court which is outside the temple and do not measure it, for it has been given to the nations; and they will tread under foot the holy city for forty-two months (3 ½ years)." **Revelation 11:2**
- "I heard the man dressed in linen, who was above the waters of the river, as he raised his right hand and his left toward heaven, and swore by Him who lives forever that it would be for a time, times, and half a time; and as soon as they finish shattering the power of the holy people, all these events will be completed (3 ½ years)." **Daniel 12:7**
- "Then the woman fled into the wilderness where she had a place prepared by God, so that there she would be nourished for one thousand two hundred and sixty days (3 ½ years)." **Revelation 12:6**

3 ½ YEARS GREAT TRIBULATION

"The prince...in the middle of the week he will put a stop to sacrifice and grain offering; and on the wing of abominations *will come* one who makes desolate, even until a complete destruction, one that is decreed, is poured out on the one who makes desolate." **Daniel 9:26, 27**

"And he will make a firm covenant with the many for one week, but in the middle of the week he will put a stop to sacrifice and grain offering; and on the wing of abominations will come one who makes desolate, even complete destruction, one that is decreed, is poured out on the one who makes desolate." Daniel 9:27

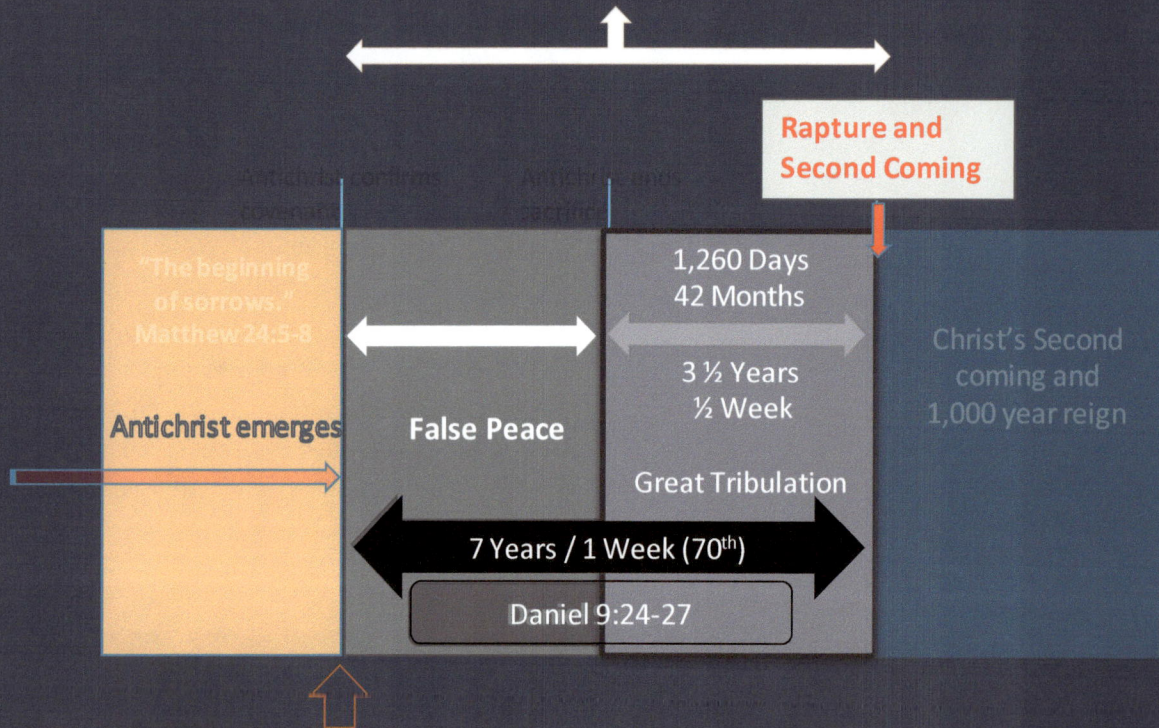

Rapture and Second Coming

Antichrist confirms covenant

Antichrist ends sacrifice

"The beginning of sorrows." Matthew 24:5-8

Antichrist emerges

False Peace

1,260 Days
42 Months

3 ½ Years
½ Week

Great Tribulation

Christ's Second coming and 1,000 year reign

7 Years / 1 Week (70th)

Daniel 9:24-27

"For you your selves know full well that the day of the Lord will come just like a thief in the night. While they are saying, "Peace and safety!" then destruction will come upon them suddenly like labor pains upon a woman with child, and they will not escape." **1 Thessalonians 5:2-3**

THE GREAT TRIBULATION (SEALS)

"When He broke the second seal…a red horse, went out; and to him who sat on it, it was granted to take peace from the earth, and that *men* would slay one another; and a great sword was given to him." **Revelation 6:3, 4**

"When the Lamb broke the fourth seal…an ashen horse; and he who sat on it had the name Death; and Hades was following with him. Authority was given to them over a fourth of the earth, to kill with sword and with famine and with pestilence and by the wild beasts of the earth." **Revelation 6:7, 8**

"When the Lamb broke the fifth seal, I saw underneath the altar the souls of those who had been slain because of the word of God, and because of the testimony which they had maintained; and they cried out with a loud voice, saying, 'How long, O Lord, holy and true, will You refrain from judging and avenging our blood on those who dwell on the earth?' And there was given to each of them a white robe; and they were told that they should rest for a little while longer, until *the number of* their fellow servants and their brethren who were to be killed even as they had been, would be completed also." **Revelation 6:9-11**

"When the Lamb broke the seventh seal…I saw the seven angels who stand before God, and seven trumpets were given to them." **Revelation 8:1, 2**

2nd Seal: War

4th Seal: Death

5th Seal: Martyrs

7th Seal: Trumpets

3 ½ YEARS GREAT TRIBULATION

Abomination of Desolation

3rd Seal: Famine

6th Seal: Terror

Continued

"When He broke the third seal…a black horse; and he who sat on it had a pair of scales in his hand. And I heard *something* like a voice…saying, 'A quart of wheat for a denarius, and three quarts of barley for a denarius." **Revelation 6:5, 6**

"I looked when He broke the sixth seal…there was a great earthquake; and the sun became black as sackcloth…the whole moon became like blood…the stars of the sky fell to the earth, as a fig tree casts its unripe figs when shaken by a great wind. The sky was split apart like a scroll when it is rolled up, and every mountain and island were moved out of their places." **Revelation 6:12, 13, 14**

THE GREAT TRIBULATION

"When the Lamb broke the seventh seal...I saw the seven angels who stand before God, and seven trumpets were given to them." **Revelation 8:1, 2**

7th Seal: Trumpets

"The second angel sounded, and *something* like a great mountain burning with fire was thrown into the sea; and a third of the sea became blood, and a third of the creatures which were in the sea and had life, died; and a third of the ships were destroyed." **Revelation 8:8-9**

2nd Trumpet: Great Burning Mountain Thrown

"The third angel sounded, and a great star fell from heaven, burning like a torch, and it fell on a third of the rivers and on the springs of waters. The name of the star is called Wormwood; and a third of the waters became wormwood, and many men died from the waters, because they were made bitter." **Revelation 8:10-11**

3rd Trumpet: Great Star Falls

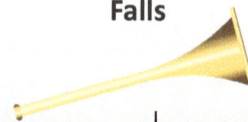

3 ½ YEARS GREAT TRIBULATION

1st Trumpet: Hail & Fire

4th Trumpet: Darkness

"The first sounded, and there came hail and fire, mixed with blood, and they were thrown to the earth; and a third of the earth was burned up, and a third of the trees were burned up, and all the green grass was burned up" **Revelation 6:7**

"The fourth angel sounded, and a third of the sun and a third of the moon and a third of the stars were struck, so that a third of them would be darkened and the day would not shine for a third of it, and the night in the same way." **Revelation 8:12**

"Then I looked, and I heard an eagle flying in midheaven, saying with a loud voice, "Woe, woe, woe to those who dwell on the earth, because of the remaining blasts of the trumpet of the three angels who are about to sound!" **Revelation 8:13**

"Then the fifth angel sounded, and I saw a star from heaven which had fallen to the earth; and the key of the bottomless pit was given to him. He opened the bottomless pit, and smoke went up out of the pit, like the smoke of a great furnace; and the sun and the air were darkened by the smoke of the pit. Then out of the smoke came locusts upon the earth, and power was given them, as the scorpions of the earth have power. They were told not to hurt the grass of the earth, nor any green thing, nor any tree, but only the men who do not have the seal of God on their foreheads."
Revelation 9:1-4

"Then the seventh angel sounded; and there were loud voices in heaven, saying, "The kingdom of the world has become *the kingdom* of our Lord and of His Christ; and He will reign forever and ever." **Revelation 11:15**

5th Trumpet: Locusts

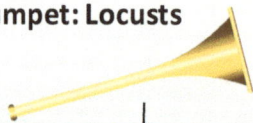

7th Trumpet: The Great Trumpet

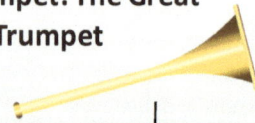

3 ½ YEARS GREAT TRIBULATION

Continued

6ᵗʰ Trumpet: 200 Million Man Army

"Then the sixth angel sounded...so that they would kill a third of mankind. The number of the armies of the horsemen was two hundred million" **Revelation 9:13-16**

SECOND COMING OF CHRIST AND RAPTURE OF THE CHURCH

LAST & GREAT TRUMPET:

- "In a moment, in the twinkling of an eye, at the last trumpet; for the trumpet will sound, and the dead will be raised imperishable, and we will be changed." **1 Corinthians 15:52**

- "But immediately after the tribulation of those days THE SUN WILL BE DARKENED, AND THE MOON WILL NOT GIVE ITS LIGHT, AND THE STARS WILL FALL from the sky, and the powers of the heavens will be shaken. "And then the sign of the Son of Man will appear in the sky, and then all the tribes of the earth will mourn, and they will see the SON OF MAN COMING ON THE CLOUDS OF THE SKY with power and great glory. And He will send forth His angels with A GREAT TRUMPET and THEY WILL GATHER TOGETHER His elect from the four winds, from one end of the sky to the other." **Matthew 24:29-31**

- "But of that day and hour no one knows, not even the angels of heaven, nor the Son, but the Father alone. For the coming of the Son of Man will be just like the days of Noah. For as in those days before the flood they were eating and drinking, marrying and giving in marriage, until the day that Noah entered the ark, and they did not understand until the flood came and took them all away; so will the coming of the Son of Man be. Then there will be two men in the field; one will be taken and one will be left. Two women *will be* grinding at the mill; one will be taken and one will be left." **Matthew 24:36-41**

7th Trumpet: The Great Trumpet

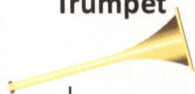

SECOND COMING OF CHRIST

"Then the seventh angel sounded; and there were loud voices in heaven, saying,
'The kingdom of the world has become *the kingdom* of our Lord and of His Christ; and He will reign forever and ever.'"
Revelation 11:15

4th Bowl: Sun Scorches Men

6th Bowl: Great River Dried Up

"The sixth *angel* poured out his bowl on the great river, the Euphrates; and its water was dried up, so that the way would be prepared for the kings from the east." **Revelation 16:12**

RAPTURE AT END OF TRIBULATION AND BEFORE THE BOWLS OF WRATH:

- "But immediately after the tribulation of those days THE SUN WILL BE DARKENED, AND THE MOON WILL NOT GIVE ITS LIGHT, AND THE STARS WILL FALL from the sky, and the powers of the heavens will be shaken. "And then the sign of the Son of Man will appear in the sky, and then all the tribes of the earth will mourn, and they will see the SON OF MAN COMING ON THE CLOUDS OF THE SKY with power and great glory. And He will send forth His angels with A GREAT TRUMPET and THEY WILL GATHER TOGETHER His elect from the four winds, from one end of the sky to the other." **Matthew 24:29-31**
- "Then they will deliver you to tribulation, and will kill you, and you will be hated by all nations because of My name." **Matthew 24:9**
- "After these things I looked, and behold, a great multitude which no one could count, from every nation and all tribes and peoples and tongues, standing before the throne and before the Lamb, clothed in white robes, and palm branches were in their hands...'These are the ones who come out of the great tribulation, and they have washed their robes and made them white in the blood of the Lamb.'" **Revelation 7:9,14**
- "And they overcame him because of the blood of the Lamb and because of the word of their testimony, and they did not love their life even when faced with death." **Revelation 12:11**
- "I kept looking, and that horn was waging war with the saints and overpowering them" **Daniel 7:21**
- "It was also given to him to make war with the saints and to overcome them, and authority over every tribe and people and tongue and nation was given to him." **Revelation 13:7**
- "He will speak out against the Most High and wear down the saints of the Highest One, and he will intend to make alterations in times and in law; and they will be given into his hand for a time, times, and half a time." **Daniel 7:25**

SECOND COMING PROCESSION

THE END TIME HARVEST:

"Jesus presented another parable to them, saying, "The kingdom of heaven may be compared to a man who sowed good seed in his field. "But while his men were sleeping, his enemy came and sowed tares among the wheat, and went away. "But when the wheat sprouted and bore grain, then the tares became evident also. "The slaves of the landowner came and said to him, 'Sir, did you not sow good seed in your field? How then does it have tares?' "And he said to them, 'An enemy has done this!' The slaves said to him, 'Do you want us, then, to go and gather them up?' "But he said, 'No; for while you are gathering up the tares, you may uproot the wheat with them. 'Allow both to grow together until the harvest; and in the time of the harvest I will say to the reapers, "First gather up the tares and bind them in bundles to burn them up; but gather the wheat into my barn." Then He left the crowds and went into the house. And His disciples came to Him and said, "Explain to us the parable of the tares of the field." And He said, "The one who sows the good seed is the Son of Man, and the field is the world; and *as for* the good seed, these are the sons of the kingdom; and the tares are the sons of the evil *one;* and the enemy who sowed them is the devil, and the harvest is the end of the age; and the reapers are angels. So just as the tares are gathered up and burned with fire, so shall it be at the end of the age. The Son of Man will send forth His angels, and they will gather out of His kingdom all stumbling blocks, and those who commit lawlessness, and will throw them into the furnace of fire; in that place there will be weeping and gnashing of teeth. Then THE RIGHTEOUS WILL SHINE FORTH AS THE SUN in the kingdom of their Father. He who has ears, let him hear." **Matthew 13:24-30, 37-43C**

7th Trumpet: The Great Trumpet

SECOND COMING OF CHRIST

"Then the seventh angel sounded; and there were loud voices in heaven, saying, 'The kingdom of the world has become *the kingdom* of our Lord and of His Christ; and He will reign forever and ever.'" **Revelation 11:15**

4th Bowl: Sun Scorches Men

6th Bowl: Great River Dried Up

"The sixth *angel* poured out his bowl on the great river, the Euphrates; and its water was dried up, so that the way would be prepared for the kings from the east." **Revelation 16:12**

SECOND COMING PROCESSION

"Then the seventh angel sounded; and there were loud voices in heaven, saying, 'The kingdom of the world has become *the kingdom* of our Lord and of His Christ; and He will reign forever and ever.'" **Revelation 11:15**

THE END TIME HARVEST:

"Then I looked, and behold, a white cloud, and sitting on the cloud *was* one like a son of man, having a golden crown on His head and a sharp sickle in His hand. And another angel came out of the temple, crying out with a loud voice to Him who sat on the cloud, 'Put in your sickle and reap, for the hour to reap has come, because the harvest of the earth is ripe.' Then He who sat on the cloud swung His sickle over the earth, and the earth was reaped. And another angel came out of the temple which is in heaven, and he also had a sharp sickle. Then another angel, the one who has power over fire, came out from the altar; and he called with a loud voice to him who had the sharp sickle, saying, 'Put in your sharp sickle and gather the clusters from the vine of the earth, because her grapes are ripe.' So the angel swung his sickle to the earth and gathered *the clusters from* the vine of the earth, and threw them into the great wine press of the wrath of God. And the wine press was trodden outside the city, and blood came out from the wine press, up to the horses' bridles, for a distance of two hundred miles." **Revelation 14:14-20**

7th Trumpet: The Great Trumpet

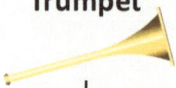

SECOND COMING OF CHRIST

1st Bowl: Sores

4th Bowl: Sun Scorches Men

6th Bowl: Great River Dried Up

"So the first *angel* went and poured out his bowl on the earth; and it became a loathsome and malignant sore on the people who had the mark of the beast and who worshiped his image" **Revelation 16:1-2**

"The sixth *angel* poured out his bowl on the great river, the Euphrates; and its water was dried up, so that the way would be prepared for the kings from the east." **Revelation 16:12**

SECOND COMING PROCESSION

"Then the seventh angel sounded; and there were loud voices in heaven, saying, 'The kingdom of the world has become *the kingdom* of our Lord and of His Christ; and He will reign forever and ever.'" **Revelation 11:15**

RAPTURE:

Receive Glorified Bodies:

- "Beloved, now we are children of God, and it has not appeared as yet what we will be. We know that when He appears, we will be like Him, because we will see Him just as He is." **1 John 3:2**
- "When Christ, who is our life, is revealed, then you also will be revealed with Him in glory." **Colossians 3:4**
- "So also is the resurrection of the dead. It is sown a perishable *body,* it is raised an imperishable *body;* it is sown in dishonor, it is raised in glory; it is sown in weakness, it is raised in power; it is sown a natural body, it is raised a spiritual body." **1 Corinthians 15:42-44**

7th Trumpet:
The Great
Trumpet

SECOND COMING OF CHRIST

4th Bowl: Sun Scorches Men

6th Bowl: Great River Dried Up

1st Bowl: Sores

"So the first *angel* went and poured out his bowl on the earth; and it became a loathsome and malignant sore on the people who had the mark of the beast and who worshiped his image" **Revelation 16:1-2**

"The sixth *angel* poured out his bowl on the great river, the Euphrates; and its water was dried up, so that the way would be prepared for the kings from the east." **Revelation 16:12**

Second Coming Process:

| Rapture | → | Sea of Glass Meeting Place | → | Return with Christ |

Purpose of the Rapture and Sea of Glass Meeting Place:

"The saints will be gathered together in the sky to **receive their resurrected bodies**, be **evaluated and rewarded by Jesus**, and then **organized** and **mobilized** for the battle of Jerusalem which results in the hostile takeover of the governments of all the nations on earth." -(Excerpt International House of Prayer, *100 Most Frequently Asked Questions About the End Times*)

References:

- "And I saw something like a sea of glass mixed with fire, and those who had been victorious over the beast and his image and the number of his name, standing on the sea of glass, holding harps of God." **Revelation 15:2**
- "And before the throne there was something like a sea of glass, like crystal; and in the center and around the throne, four living creatures full of eyes in front and behind." **Revelation 4:6**
- "A river of fire was flowing
    And coming out from before Him;
    Thousands upon thousands were attending Him,
    And myriads upon myriads were standing before Him;
    The court sat,
    And the books were opened." **Daniel 7:10**

> Purpose of Rapture and Sea of Glass Meeting Place:
> - **Receive Resurrected Bodies**
> - **Evaluated and Rewarded by Jesus**
> - **Organize**
> - **Mobilize**

Sea of Glass References:

- "And I saw something like a sea of glass mixed with fire, and those who had been victorious over the beast and his image and the number of his name, standing on the sea of glass, holding harps of God." **Revelation 15:2**
- "And before the throne there was something like a sea of glass, like crystal; and in the center and around the throne, four living creatures full of eyes in front and behind." **Revelation 4:6**
- "A river of fire was flowing

   And coming out from before Him;

   Thousands upon thousands were attending Him,

   And myriads upon myriads were standing before Him;

   The court sat,

   And the books were opened." **Daniel 7:10**
- "And the twelve gates were twelve pearls; each one of the gates was a single pearl. And the street of the city was pure gold, like transparent glass." **Revelation 21:21**
- "And they saw the God of Israel; and under His feet there appeared to be a pavement of sapphire, as clear as the sky itself." **Exodus 24:10**

THE VICTORIOUS CHURCH

"And they overcame him because of the blood of the Lamb and because of the word of their testimony, and they did not love their life even when faced with death."
Revelation 12:11

THE VICTORIOUS CHURCH:

- "Those who have insight will shine brightly like the brightness of the expanse of heaven, and those who lead the many to righteousness, like the stars forever and ever." **Daniel 12:3**
- "Those who have insight among the people will give understanding to the many; yet they will fall by sword and by flame, by captivity and by plunder for many days." **Daniel 11:33**
- "Now when they fall they will be granted a little help, and many will join with them in hypocrisy. Some of those who have insight will fall, in order to refine, purge and make them pure until the end time; because *it is* still *to come* at the appointed time." **Daniel 11:34-35**
- "For Zion's sake I will not keep silent, And for Jerusalem's sake I will not keep quiet, Until her righteousness goes forth like brightness, And her salvation like a torch that is burning." **Isaiah 62:1**
- "Then the kingdom of heaven will be comparable to ten virgins, who took their lamps and went out to meet the bridegroom...and five were prudent...the prudent took oil in flasks along with their lamps." **Matthew 25:1-3**

The Abomination of Desolation

3 ½ YEARS GREAT TRIBULATION

"The prince...in the middle of the week he will put a stop to sacrifice and grain offering; and on the wing of abominations *will come* one who makes desolate, even until a complete destruction, one that is decreed, is poured out on the one who makes desolate." **Daniel 9:26,27**

VICTORIOUS CHURCH: END TIME BRIDAL PARADIGM

"It will come about in that day," declares the LORD, "That you will call Me Ishi (Husband) And will no longer call Me Baali (Master)." **Hosea 2:16**

LOVE BASED OBEDIENCE:

- "He who has My commandments and keeps them is the one who loves Me; and he who loves Me will be loved by My Father, and I will love him and will disclose Myself to him." **John 14:21**
- "If you keep My commandments, you will abide in My love; just as I have kept My Father's commandments and abide in His love." **John 15:10**
- "For this is the love of God, that we keep His commandments; and His commandments are not burdensome." **1 John 5:3**
- "That He would grant you, according to the riches of His glory, to be strengthened with power through His Spirit in the inner man, so that Christ may dwell in your hearts through faith; *and* that you, being rooted and grounded in love, may be able to comprehend with all the saints what is the breadth and length and height and depth, and to know the love of Christ which surpasses knowledge, that you may be filled up to all the fullness of God." **Ephesians 3:16-20**
- "The Spirit and the bride say, "Come." **Revelation 22:17**
- "For the anxious longing of the creation waits eagerly for the revealing of the sons of God." **Romans 8:19**

The Abomination of Desolation

3 ½ YEARS GREAT TRIBULATION

"The prince...in the middle of the week he will put a stop to sacrifice and grain offering; and on the wing of abominations *will come* one who makes desolate, even until a complete destruction, one that is decreed, is poured out on the one who makes desolate." **Daniel 9:26,27**

VICTORIOUS CHURCH: END TIME PRAYER MOVEMENT

"When He had taken the book, the four living creatures and the twenty-four elders fell down before the Lamb, each one holding a harp and golden bowls full of incense, which are the prayers of the saints."
Revelation 5:8

PRAYER MOVEMENT:

- "The Spirit and the bride say, "Come." **Revelation 22:17**
- "On your walls, O Jerusalem, I have appointed watchmen; All day and all night they will never keep silent. You who remind the LORD, take no rest for yourselves; And give Him no rest until He establishes And makes Jerusalem a praise in the earth." **Isaiah 62:6-7**
- "Behold, the former things have come to pass, Now I declare new things; Before they spring forth I proclaim *them* to you. Sing to the LORD a new song, *Sing* His praise from the end of the earth! You who go down to the sea, and all that is in it. You islands, and those who dwell on them. Let the wilderness and its cities lift up *their voices,* The settlements where Kedar inhabits. Let the inhabitants of Sela sing aloud, Let them shout for joy from the tops of the mountains." **Isaiah 42:9-11**
- "For from the rising of the sun even to its setting, My name will be great among the nations, and in every place incense is going to be offered to My name, and a grain offering that is pure; for My name will be great among the nations, says the LORD of hosts." **Malachi 1:11**

The Abomination of Desolation

3 ½ YEARS GREAT TRIBULATION

"The prince...in the middle of the week he will put a stop to sacrifice and grain offering; and on the wing of abominations *will come* one who makes desolate, even until a complete destruction, one that is decreed, is poured out on the one who makes desolate." **Daniel 9:26,27**

VICTORIOUS CHURCH: END TIME EVANGELISM MOVEMENT

"This gospel of the kingdom shall be preached in the whole world as a testimony to all the nations, and then the end will come." **Matthew 24:14**

EVANGELISM MOVEMENT:

- "The gospel must first be preached to all the nations." **Mark 13:10**
- "And I saw another angel flying in midheaven, having an eternal gospel to preach to those who live on the earth, and to every nation and tribe and tongue and people;" **Revelation 14:6**
- "This gospel of the kingdom shall be preached in the whole world as a testimony to all the nations, and then the end will come." **Matthew 24:14**
- "He said, 'I am A VOICE OF ONE CRYING IN THE WILDERNESS, MAKE STRAIGHT THE WAY OF THE LORD,' as Isaiah the prophet said.'" **John 1:23**

The Abomination of Desolation

3 ½ YEARS GREAT TRIBULATION

"The prince...in the middle of the week he will put a stop to sacrifice and grain offering; and on the wing of abominations *will come* one who makes desolate, even until a complete destruction, one that is decreed, is poured out on the one who makes desolate." **Daniel 9:26,27**

VICTORIOUS CHURCH: END TIME PROPHETIC MOVEMENT

"It will come about after this That I will pour out My Spirit on all mankind; And your sons and daughters will prophesy, Your old men will dream dreams, Your young men will see visions." **Joel 2:28**

PROPHETIC MOVEMENT:

- "'AND IT SHALL BE IN THE LAST DAYS,' God says, 'THAT I WILL POUR FORTH OF MY SPIRIT ON ALL MANKIND; AND YOUR SONS AND YOUR DAUGHTERS SHALL PROPHESY, AND YOUR YOUNG MEN SHALL SEE VISIONS, AND YOUR OLD MEN SHALL DREAM DREAMS;'" **Acts 2:17**
- "And I will grant *authority* to my two witnesses, and they will prophesy for twelve hundred and sixty days, clothed in sackcloth. These are the two olive trees and the two lampstands that stand before the Lord of the earth. And if anyone wants to harm them, fire flows out of their mouth and devours their enemies; so if anyone wants to harm them, he must be killed in this way. These have the power to shut up the sky, so that rain will not fall during the days of their prophesying; and they have power over the waters to turn them into blood, and to strike the earth with every plague, as often as they desire." **Revelation 11:3-6**
- "And He answered and said, 'Elijah is coming and will restore all things;'" **Matthew 17:11**
- "Behold, I am going to send you Elijah the prophet before the coming of the great and terrible day of the LORD. He will restore the hearts of the fathers to *their* children and the hearts of the children to their fathers, so that I will not come and smite the land with a curse." **Malachi 4:5-6**

The Abomination of Desolation

3 ½ YEARS GREAT TRIBULATION

"The prince...in the middle of the week he will put a stop to sacrifice and grain offering; and on the wing of abominations *will come* one who makes desolate, even until a complete destruction, one that is decreed, is poured out on the one who makes desolate." **Daniel 9:26,27**

THE PURPOSE OF THE TRIBULATION

This is the proclamation of heaven in the context of Jesus opening up the book of the end time plan; demonstrating that the purpose of the great tribulation is for Christ to take possession of what He paid for at the cross, the salvation of man. His strategy is to use the least severe means to save the most people, at the deepest level of love.

"When He had taken the book, the four living creatures and the twenty-four elders fell down before the Lamb, each one holding a harp and golden bowls full of incense, which are the prayers of the saints. And they sang a new song, saying, 'Worthy are You to take the book and to break its seals; for You were slain, and purchased for God with Your blood men from every tribe and tongue and people and nation. You have made them to be a kingdom and priests to our God; and they will reign upon the earth.'" **Revelation 5:8-10**

- "At night my soul longs for You, Indeed, my spirit within me seeks You diligently; For when the earth experiences Your judgments The inhabitants of the world learn righteousness." **Isaiah 26:9**
- "The anger of the LORD will not turn back until He has performed and carried out the purposes of His heart; in the last days you will clearly understand it." **Jeremiah 23:20**
- "The Lord is not slow about His promise, as some count slowness, but is patient toward you, not wishing for any to perish but for all to come to repentance." **2 Peter 3:9**

"From the time that the regular sacrifice is abolished and the abomination of desolation is set up, there will be 1,290 days." **Daniel 12:11**

"Then the seventh angel sounded; and there were loud voices in heaven, saying, '"The kingdom of the world has become *the kingdom* of our Lord and of His Christ; and He will reign forever and ever.'" **Revelation 11:15**

7th Trumpet: The Great Trumpet

"So the first *angel* went and poured out his bowl on the earth; and it became a loathsome and malignant sore on the people who had the mark of the beast and who worshiped his image" **Revelation 16:1-2**

1st Bowl: Sores

"The second *angel* poured out his bowl into the sea, and it became blood like *that* of a dead man; and every living thing in the sea died." **Revelation 16:3**

2nd Bowl: Sea Becomes Blood

"Then the third *angel* poured out his bowl into the rivers and the springs of waters; and they became blood." **Revelation 16:4**

3rd Bowl: Rivers and Springs Become Blood

SECOND COMING OF CHRIST

SECOND COMING OF CHRIST: BOWLS FIRST 30 DAY TRANSITION INTO MILLENNIAL KINGDOM

"The fourth *angel* poured out his bowl upon the sun, and it was given to it to scorch men with fire." **Revelation 16:8**

"Then the fifth *angel* poured out his bowl on the throne of the beast, and his kingdom became darkened; and they gnawed their tongues because of pain." **Revelation 16:10**

"Then the seventh *angel* poured out his bowl upon the air, and a loud voice came out of the temple from the throne, saying, 'It is done.'" **Revelation 16:17**

4th Bowl: Sun Scorches Men

5th Bowl: Beast's Kingdom Darkened

7th Bowl: It is Done

SECOND COMING OF CHRIST   Continued

6th Bowl: Great River Dried

"The sixth *angel* poured out his bowl on the great river, the Euphrates; and its water was dried up, so that the way would be prepared for the kings from the east." **Revelation 16:12**

SECOND COMING PROCESSION

> "Then the seventh angel sounded; and there were loud voices in heaven, saying,
> 'The kingdom of the world has become *the kingdom* of our Lord and of His Christ; and He will reign forever and ever.'" **Revelation 11:15**

7th Trumpet: The Great Trumpet

Second Coming Procession:

- "And I saw heaven opened, and behold, a white horse, and He who sat on it *is* called Faithful and True, and in righteousness He judges and wages war. His eyes *are* a flame of fire, and on His head *are* many diadems; and He has a name written *on Him* which no one knows except Himself. *He is* clothed with a robe dipped in blood, and His name is called The Word of God. And the armies which are in heaven, clothed in fine linen, white *and* clean, were following Him on white horses. From His mouth comes a sharp sword, so that with it He may strike down the nations, and He will rule them with a rod of iron; and He treads the wine press of the fierce wrath of God, the Almighty. And on His robe and on His thigh He has a name written, KING OF KINGS, AND LORD OF LORDS." **Revelation 19:11-16**
- "I kept looking, and that horn was waging war with the saints and overpowering them until the Ancient of Days came and judgment was passed in favor of the saints of the Highest One, and the time arrived when the saints took possession of the kingdom." **Daniel 7:21-22**
- "But the saints of the Highest One will receive the kingdom and possess the kingdom forever, for all ages to come." **Daniel 7:18**
- "Does any one of you, when he has a case against his neighbor, dare to go to law before the unrighteous and not before the saints? Or do you not know that the saints will judge the world? If the world is judged by you, are you not competent *to constitute* the smallest law courts? Do you not know that we will judge angels? How much more matters of this life?" **1 Corinthians 6:1-3**

SECOND COMING OF CHRIST PROCESSION　　　　Continued

SECOND COMING PROCESSION FROM EGYPT TO THE MOUNT OF OLIVES

Second Coming Procession:

- "The oracle concerning Egypt. Behold, the LORD is riding on a swift cloud and is about to come to Egypt; The idols of Egypt will tremble at His presence, And the heart of the Egyptians will melt within them." **Isaiah 19:1**
- "Who is this who comes from Edom, With garments of glowing colors from Bozrah, This One who is majestic in His apparel, Marching in the greatness of His strength? It is I who speak in righteousness, mighty to save. Why is Your apparel red, And Your garments like the one who treads in the wine press? I have trodden the wine trough alone, And from the peoples there was no man with Me I also trod them in My anger And trampled them in My wrath And their lifeblood is sprinkled on My garments And I stained all My raiment. For the day of vengeance was in My heart, And My year of redemption has come. I looked, and there was no one to help And I was astonished and there was no one to uphold; So My own arm brought salvation to Me, And My wrath upheld Me. I trod down the peoples in My anger And made them drunk in My wrath, And I poured out their lifeblood on the earth." **Isaiah 63:1-6**
- "Egypt will become a waste, And Edom will become a desolate wilderness, Because of the violence done to the sons of Judah, In whose land they have shed innocent blood." **Joel 3:19**
- "God comes from Teman, And the Holy One from Mount Paran. Selah. His splendor covers the heavens, And the earth is full of His praise." **Habakkuk 3:3**
- "Whoever then annuls one of the least of these commandments, and teaches others to do the same, shall be called least in the kingdom of heaven; but whoever keeps and teaches them, he shall be called great in the kingdom of heaven." **Matthew 5:19**
- "*It was* also about these men *that* Enoch, *in* the seventh *generation* from Adam, prophesied, saying, "Behold, the Lord came with many thousands of His holy ones, to execute judgment upon all, and to convict all the ungodly of all their ungodly deeds which they have done in an ungodly way, and of all the harsh things which ungodly sinners have spoken against Him." **Jude 1:14-15**

SECOND COMING PROCESSION FROM EGYPT TO THE MOUNT OF OLIVES: The Day of The Lord

> "Then the seventh angel sounded; and there were loud voices in heaven, saying, 'The kingdom of the world has become *the kingdom* of our Lord and of His Christ; and He will reign forever and ever.'" **Revelation 11:15**

Day of the Lord:

"I will gather all the nations
And bring them down to the valley of Jehoshaphat.
Then I will enter into judgment with them there
On behalf of My people and My inheritance, Israel,
Whom they have scattered among the nations;
And they have divided up My land...
Hasten and come, all you surrounding nations,
And gather yourselves there.
Bring down, O LORD, Your mighty ones.
Let the nations be aroused
And come up to the valley of Jehoshaphat,
For there I will sit to judge
All the surrounding nations.
Put in the sickle, for the harvest is ripe.
Come, tread, for the wine press is full;
The vats overflow, for their wickedness is great.
Multitudes, multitudes in the valley of decision!
For the day of the LORD is near in the valley of decision."
Joel 3:2, 11-14

SECOND COMING OF CHRIST PROCESSION   Continued

Day of the Lord:

"LORD, I have heard the report about You *and* I fear. O LORD, revive Your work in the midst of the years, In the midst of the years make it known; In wrath remember mercy. God comes from Teman, And the Holy One from Mount Paran. Selah. His splendor covers the heavens, And the earth is full of His praise. *His* radiance is like the sunlight; He has rays *flashing* from His hand, And there is the hiding of His power. Before Him goes pestilence, And plague comes after Him. He stood and surveyed the earth; He looked and startled the nations. Yes, the perpetual mountains were shattered, The ancient hills collapsed. His ways are everlasting. I saw the tents of Cushan under distress, The tent curtains of the land of Midian were trembling. Did the LORD rage against the rivers, Or *was* Your anger against the rivers, Or *was* Your wrath against the sea, That You rode on Your horses, On Your chariots of salvation? Your bow was made bare, The rods of chastisement were sworn. Selah. You cleaved the earth with rivers. The mountains saw You *and* quaked; The downpour of waters swept by. The deep uttered forth its voice, It lifted high its hands. Sun *and* moon stood in their places; They went away at the light of Your arrows, At the radiance of Your gleaming spear. In indignation You marched through the earth; In anger You trampled the nations. You went forth for the salvation of Your people, For the salvation of Your anointed. You struck the head of the house of the evil To lay him open from thigh to neck. Selah. You pierced with his own spears The head of his throngs. They stormed in to scatter us; Their exultation *was* like those Who devour the oppressed in secret. You trampled on the sea with Your horses, On the surge of many waters. I heard and my inward parts trembled, At the sound my lips quivered. Decay enters my bones, And in my place I tremble. Because I must wait quietly for the day of distress, For the people to arise *who* will invade us." **Habakkuk 3:2-16**

Day of the Lord:

"Why are the nations in an uproar And the peoples devising a vain thing? The kings of the earth take their stand And the rulers take counsel together Against the LORD and against His Anointed, saying, "Let us tear their fetters apart And cast away their cords from us!" He who sits in the heavens laughs, The Lord scoffs at them. Then He will speak to them in His anger And terrify them in His fury, saying, "But as for Me, I have installed My King Upon Zion, My holy mountain." "I will surely tell of the decree of the LORD: He said to Me, 'You are My Son, Today I have begotten You. 'Ask of Me, and I will surely give the nations as Your inheritance, And the *very* ends of the earth as Your possession. 'You shall break them with a rod of iron, You shall shatter them like earthenware.'" Now therefore, O kings, show discernment; Take warning, O judges of the earth. Worship the LORD with reverence And rejoice with trembling. Do homage to the Son, that He not become angry, and you perish *in* the way, For His wrath may soon be kindled. How blessed are all who take refuge in Him!" **Psalm 2:1-12**

"And I saw heaven opened, and behold, a white horse, and He who sat on it *is* called Faithful and True, and in righteousness He judges and wages war. His eyes *are* a flame of fire, and on His head *are* many diadems; and He has a name written *on Him* which no one knows except Himself. *He is* clothed with a robe dipped in blood, and His name is called The Word of God. And the armies which are in heaven, clothed in fine linen, white *and* clean, were following Him on white horses. From His mouth comes a sharp sword, so that with it He may strike down the nations, and He will rule them with a rod of iron; and He treads the wine press of the fierce wrath of God, the Almighty. And on His robe and on His thigh He has a name written, 'KING OF KINGS, AND LORD OF LORDS.' Then I saw an angel standing in the sun, and he cried out with a loud voice, saying to all the birds which fly in midheaven, "Come, assemble for the great supper of God, so that you may eat the flesh of kings and the flesh of commanders and the flesh of mighty men and the flesh of horses and of those who sit on them and the flesh of all men, both free men and slaves, and small and great." And I saw the beast and the kings of the earth and their armies assembled to make war against Him who sat on the horse and against His army. And the beast was seized, and with him the false prophet who performed the signs in his presence, by which he deceived those who had received the mark of the beast and those who worshiped his image; these two were thrown alive into the lake of fire which burns with brimstone. And the rest were killed with the sword which came from the mouth of Him who sat on the horse, and all the birds were filled with their flesh." **Revelation 19:11-21**

SECOND COMING PROCESSION FROM EGYPT TO THE MOUNT OF OLIVES: The Day of The Lord

Day of the Lord: Winepress

- "Therefore wait for Me," declares the LORD, "For the day when I rise up as a witness. Indeed, My decision is to gather nations, To assemble kingdoms, To pour out on them My indignation, All My burning anger; For all the earth will be devoured By the fire of My zeal." **Zephaniah 3:8**
- "I have trodden the wine trough alone, And from the peoples there was no man with Me. I also trod them in My anger And trampled them in My wrath; And their lifeblood is sprinkled on My garments, And I stained all My raiment." **Isaiah 63:3**
- "From His mouth comes a sharp sword, so that with it He may strike down the nations, and He will rule them with a rod of iron; and He treads the wine press of the fierce wrath of God, the Almighty." **Revelation 19:15**
- "Put in the sickle, for the harvest is ripe. Come, tread, for the wine press is full; The vats overflow, for their wickedness is great." **Joel 3:13**

"Then the seventh angel sounded; and there were loud voices in heaven, saying,
'The kingdom of the world has become *the kingdom* of our Lord and of His Christ; and He will reign forever and ever.'"
Revelation 11:15

SECOND COMING OF CHRIST PROCESSION   **Continued**

ONE WORLD RELIGION: THE HARLOT BABYLON AND THE FALSE PROPHET

- "Then one of the seven angels who had the seven bowls came and spoke with me, saying, 'Come here, I will show you the judgment of the great harlot who sits on many waters, with whom the kings of the earth committed *acts of* immorality, and those who dwell on the earth were made drunk with the wine of her immorality.' And he carried me away in the Spirit into a wilderness; and I saw a woman sitting on a scarlet beast, full of blasphemous names, having seven heads and ten horns. The woman was clothed in purple and scarlet, and adorned with gold and precious stones and pearls, having in her hand a gold cup full of abominations and of the unclean things of her immorality, and on her forehead a name *was* written, a mystery, 'BABYLON THE GREAT, THE MOTHER OF HARLOTS AND OF THE ABOMINATIONS OF THE EARTH.' And I saw the woman drunk with the blood of the saints, and with the blood of the witnesses of Jesus. When I saw her, I wondered greatly. And the angel said to me, 'Why do you wonder? I will tell you the mystery of the woman and of the beast that carries her, which has the seven heads and the ten horns…The woman whom you saw is the great city, which reigns over the kings of the earth.'" **Revelation 17:1-7, 18**
- "And the devil who deceived them was thrown into the lake of fire and brimstone, where the beast and the false prophet are also; and they will be tormented day and night forever and ever." **Revelation 20:10**
- "Beware of the false prophets, who come to you in sheep's clothing, but inwardly are ravenous wolves." **Matthew 7:15**
- "For false Christs and false prophets will arise and will show great signs and wonders, so as to mislead, if possible, even the elect." **Matthew 24:24**
- "That is, the one whose coming is in accord with the activity of Satan, with all power and signs and false wonders," **2 Thessalonians 2:9**

Note: When a harlot was mentioned in the Old Testament, and was not talking about a person, it is a direct reference to idolatry (false religion, false God, idol worship, demonic activity).

ONE WORLD RELIGION: THE HARLOT BABYLON AND THE FALSE PROPHET

- "Then I saw another beast (false prophet) coming up out of the earth; and he had two horns like a lamb and he spoke as a dragon. He exercises all the authority of the first beast in his presence. And he makes the earth and those who dwell in it to worship the first beast, whose fatal wound was healed. He performs great signs, so that he even makes fire come down out of heaven to the earth in the presence of men. And he deceives those who dwell on the earth because of the signs which it was given him to perform in the presence of the beast, telling those who dwell on the earth to make an image to the beast who had the wound of the sword and has come to life. And it was given to him to give breath to the image of the beast, so that the image of the beast would even speak and cause as many as do not worship the image of the beast to be killed. And he causes all, the small and the great, and the rich and the poor, and the free men and the slaves, to be given a mark on their right hand or on their forehead, and *he provides* that no one will be able to buy or to sell, except the one who has the mark, *either* the name of the beast or the number of his name." **Revelation 13:11-17**
- "And I saw *coming* out of the mouth of the dragon and out of the mouth of the beast and out of the mouth of the false prophet, three unclean spirits like frogs; for they are spirits of demons, performing signs, which go out to the kings of the whole world, to gather them together for the war of the great day of God, the Almighty." **Revelation 16:13-14**

Old Testament References:

- "Moreover, you played the harlot with the Assyrians because you were not satisfied; you played the harlot with them and still were not satisfied." **Ezekiel 16:28**
- "God says, 'If a husband divorces his wife And she goes from him And belongs to another man, Will he still return to her? Will not that land be completely polluted? But you are a harlot with many lovers; Yet you turn to Me,' declares the LORD." **Jeremiah 3:1**
- "For long ago I broke your yoke And tore off your bonds; But you said, 'I will not serve!' For on every high hill And under every green tree You have lain down as a harlot.'" **Jeremiah 2:20**
- "How the faithful city has become a harlot, She who was full of justice! Righteousness once lodged in her, But now murderers." **Isaiah 1:21**
- "For their mother has played the harlot; She who conceived them has acted shamefully. For she said, 'I will go after my lovers, Who give *me* my bread and my water, My wool and my flax, my oil and my drink.'" **Hosea 2:5**

PRE-TRIBULATION RAPTURE ARGUMENTS

Part of the Gospel is that we will not go through the tribulation.

"For God so loved the world, that He gave His only begotten Son, that whoever believes in Him shall not perish, but have eternal life. "For God did not send the Son into the world to judge the world, but that the world might be saved through Him. "He who believes in Him is not judged; he who does not believe has been judged already, because he has not believed in the name of the only begotten Son of God. "This is the judgment, that the Light has come into the world, and men loved the darkness rather than the Light, for their deeds were evil. "For everyone who does evil hates the Light, and does not come to the Light for fear that his deeds will be exposed. "But he who practices the truth comes to the Light, so that his deeds may be manifested as having been wrought in God." **John 3:16-21**

"Much more then, having now been justified by His blood, we shall be saved from the wrath *of God* through Him. For if while we were enemies we were reconciled to God through the death of His Son, much more, having been reconciled, we shall be saved by His life. And not only this, but we also exult in God through our Lord Jesus Christ, through whom we have now received the reconciliation." **Romans 5:9-11**

The gospel is the good news that we were sinners, enemies of God, and the wrath of God was toward us, but Jesus Christ died and satisfied that wrath and was resurrected on the third day. We now have peace with God by grace through faith in Jesus by repenting of our sins. We no longer have to face the wrath of hell or the wrath of the day of the Lord. However, the gospel does not promise we will not have to endure Satan's wrath.

What about Revelation 3:10?

"Because you have kept the word of My perseverance, I also will keep you from the hour of testing, that hour which is about to come upon the whole world, to test those who dwell on the earth." **Revelation 3:10**

- The word "from" is the same word used in **John 17:15**, "I do not ask You to take them out of the world, but to keep them from the evil one."

Jesus states clearly that the idea is not for the Father to take us out of the world, but that the Father would "preserve" us from the "evil one."

"That He might present to Himself the church in all her glory, having no spot or wrinkle or any such thing; but that she would be holy and blameless." **Ephesians 5:27**

- This message was to the actual church of Philadelphia, therefore, either the whole church backslid or this verse is not referring to the rapture.

PRE-TRIBULATION RAPTURE ARGUMENTS

God loves us too much to allow us to go through the tribulation.

- "But the one who endures to the end, he will be saved." **Matthew 24:13**
- "For I will show him how much he (Paul) must suffer for My name's sake." **Acts 9:16**
- "Truly, truly, I say to you, when you were younger, you used to gird yourself and walk wherever you wished; but when you grow old, you will stretch out your hands and someone else will gird you, and bring you where you do not wish to go." **John 21:18** (Pointing to his martyrdom)
- "Saul was in hearty agreement with putting him to death. And on that day a great persecution began against the church in Jerusalem, and they were all scattered throughout the regions of Judea and Samaria, except the apostles." **Acts 8:1**
  - ➤ People are currently being martyred
  - ➤ Most of the Apostles were martyred, and all were severely persecuted

God does indeed love us with a perfect love. The judgments of the great tribulation are not directed toward the church, they are poured out on the antichrist's kingdom. The rage of Satan is after the church.

- "And if children, heirs also, heirs of God and fellow heirs with Christ, if indeed we suffer with Him so that we may also be glorified with Him." **Romans 8:17**
- "That I may know Him and the power of His resurrection and the fellowship of His sufferings, being conformed to His death;" **Philippians 3:10**
- "For just as the sufferings of Christ are ours in abundance, so also our comfort is abundant through Christ." **2 Corinthians 1:5**
- "I kept looking, and that horn was waging war with the saints and overpowering them." **Daniel 7:21**
- "It was also given to him to make war with the saints and to overcome them, and authority over every tribe and people and tongue and nation was given to him." **Revelation 13:7**

PRE-TRIBULATION RAPTURE ARGUMENTS

The church is mentioned in the first three chapters of Revelation, but then when the seals are opened and the tribulation begins the church is not mentioned again until it comes back to earth with Jesus Christ in Revelation 19.

There are different names given to the redeemed who comprise the church (i.e. saints, prophets, bond-servants, His servants, the ones with their robes washed, those who hold to the testimony of Jesus etc.).

- "And I saw the woman drunk with the blood of the saints, and with the blood of the witnesses of Jesus. When I saw her, I wondered greatly." **Revelation 17:6**
- "For they poured out the blood of saints and prophets, and You have given them blood to drink. They deserve it." **Revelation 16:6**
- "And the nations were enraged, and Your wrath came, and the time came for the dead to be judged, and the time to reward Your bond-servants the prophets and the saints and those who fear Your name, the small and the great, and to destroy those who destroy the earth." **Revelation 11:18**
- "But in the days of the voice of the seventh angel, when he is about to sound, then the mystery of God is finished, as He preached to His servants the prophets." **Revelation 10:7**
- "After these things I looked, and behold, a great multitude which no one could count, from every nation and *all* tribes and peoples and tongues, standing before the throne and before the Lamb, clothed in white robes, and palm branches *were* in their hands...Then one of the elders answered, saying to me, 'These who are clothed in the white robes, who are they, and where have they come from?' I said to him, 'My lord, you know.' And he said to me, 'These are the ones who come out of the great tribulation, and they have washed their robes and made them white in the blood of the Lamb.'" **Revelation 7:9,13-14**
- "When the Lamb broke the fifth seal, I saw underneath the altar the souls of those who had been slain because of the word of God, and because of the testimony which they had maintained; and they cried out with a loud voice, saying, 'How long, O Lord, holy and true, will You refrain from judging and avenging our blood on those who dwell on the earth?' And there was given to each of them a white robe; and they were told that they should rest for a little while longer, until *the number of* their fellow servants and their brethren who were to be killed even as they had been, would be completed also." **Revelation 6:9-11**
- "So the dragon was enraged with the woman, and went off to make war with the rest of her children, who keep the commandments of God and hold to the testimony of Jesus." **Revelation 12:17**

PRE-TRIBULATION RAPTURE ARGUMENTS

We are not appointed to wrath.
"For God has not destined us for wrath, but for obtaining salvation through our Lord Jesus Christ," **1 Thessalonians 5:9,** and "to wait for His Son from heaven, whom He raised from the dead, that is Jesus, who rescues us from the wrath to come." **1 Thessalonians 1:10**

All the judgments released in the book of Revelation are released on the antichrist, not on the church, and the bowls of wrath do not begin until after the seventh trumpet when the church will be raptured.

Also, the day of the Lord is the day of the Lord's wrath and we will return with Him. Elijah has to come before the day of the Lord and he comes for 3 ½ years during the tribulation.

- "Behold, I am going to send you Elijah the prophet before the coming of the great and terrible day of the LORD." **Malachi 4:5**
- "And I will grant *authority* to my two witnesses, and they will prophesy for twelve hundred and sixty days (3 ½ years), clothed in sackcloth. These are the two olive trees and the two lampstands that stand before the Lord of the earth. And if anyone wants to harm them, fire flows out of their mouth and devours their enemies; so if anyone wants to harm them, he must be killed in this way. These have the power to shut up the sky, so that rain will not fall during the days of their prophesying; and they have power over the waters to turn them into blood, and to strike the earth with every plague, as often as they desire." **Revelation 11:3-6**

Noah escaped God's judgment, so did Rahab, Lot, the Hebrews in Egypt and others.

- Correct, all of these escaped the judgment of God; however, all were present during the judgment of God that was poured out on those around them. Noah went through the flood, Rahab went through the battle of Jericho, Lot was present on earth and saw the cities destroyed, and the Hebrew people had to put the blood of the lamb on their doorposts in order for the judgment of God to pass over their home. They were all preserved through the judgments of God. Most pre-tribulation theologians will willingly admit that their beliefs are based solely on implications; however, there are many post-tribulation rapture scriptures that are explicit.

PRE-TRIBULATION RAPTURE ARGUMENTS

The tribulation focus is on Israel, and if the church was going to go through the rapture, than why are they not given survival instructions.

These arguments are based on false notions about the purpose of the tribulation. The purpose of the tribulation is not solely about Israel nor is it simply about surviving. It is about Jesus claiming what He purchased on the cross. How he will accomplish this is by using the least severe means to save the most people at the deepest level of love. Take note of what heaven has to say when Jesus is about to open up the book of the end-time plan.

"When He had taken the book, the four living creatures and the twenty-four elders fell down before the Lamb, each one holding a harp and golden bowls full of incense, which are the prayers of the saints. And they sang a new song, saying, "Worthy are You to take the book and to break its seals; for You were slain, and purchased for God with Your blood men from every tribe and tongue and people and nation. "You have made them to be a kingdom and priests to our God; and they will reign upon the earth." **Revelation 5:8-10**

The great tribulation is the merging of the fullness of the gentiles with the full inclusion of Israel. The full inclusion of Israel progressively builds up to the second coming of Christ.

- "For I do not want you, brethren, to be uninformed of this mystery-- so that you will not be wise in your own estimation-- that a partial hardening has happened to Israel until the fullness of the Gentiles has come in;" **Romans 11:25**
- "After these things I looked, and behold, a great multitude which no one could count, from every nation and *all* tribes and peoples and tongues, standing before the throne and before the Lamb, clothed in white robes, and palm branches *were* in their hands...Then one of the elders answered, saying to me, "These who are clothed in the white robes, who are they, and where have they come from? I said to him, "My lord, you know." And he said to me, "These are the ones who come out of the great tribulation, and they have washed their robes and made them white in the blood of the Lamb." **Revelation 7:9,13-14**
- "And so all Israel will be saved; just as it is written, "THE DELIVERER WILL COME FROM ZION, HE WILL REMOVE UNGODLINESS FROM JACOB." **Romans 11:26**
- "And they (Israel) will fall by the edge of the sword, and will be led captive into all the nations; and Jerusalem will be trampled under foot by the Gentiles until the times of the Gentiles are fulfilled." **Luke 21:24**

PRE-TRIBULATION RAPTURE ARGUMENTS

How can you be comforted if you are waiting on the antichrist and the great tribulation?

The same way Paul found comfort when he knew that he was about to be martyred, or the way that Peter and John were willing to face the consequences of their faith, they still could not refrain from preaching the gospel of Jesus Christ. Also, these signs are meant to bring hope and comfort in the knowledge that our redemption draws near.

- "For I am already being poured out as a drink offering, and the time of my departure has come. I have fought the good fight, I have finished the course, I have kept the faith; in the future there is laid up for me the crown of righteousness, which the Lord, the righteous Judge, will award to me on that day; and not only to me, but also to all who have loved His appearing." **2 Timothy 4:6-8**
- "But Peter and John answered and said to them, "Whether it is right in the sight of God to give heed to you rather than to God, you be the judge; for we cannot stop speaking about what we have seen and heard." When they had threatened them further, they let them go (finding no basis on which to punish them) on account of the people, because they were all glorifying God for what had happened; for the man was more than forty years old on whom this miracle of healing had been performed." **Acts 4:19-21**
- "But when these things begin to take place, straighten up and lift up your heads, because your redemption is drawing near." **Luke 21:28**

What about Luke 21:36?

"Watch ye therefore, and pray always, that ye may be accounted worthy to escape all these things that shall come to pass, and to stand before the Son of man." KJV

Most translations use the phrase "that you may have strength to escape." Why would we need strength if we are not going to go through the tribulation? We need supernatural strength to be faithful and persevere through the tribulation.

"But keep on the alert at all times, praying that you may have strength to escape all these things that are about to take place, and to stand before the Son of Man." **Luke 21:36**

PRE-TRIBULATION RAPTURE ARGUMENTS

How do we explain Matthew 24:36? "But of that day and hour no one knows, not even the angels of heaven, nor the Son, but the Father alone."

Up to this time only the Father knows when the Son is coming; however in the generation that the Lord returns, there will be a remnant to whom the Lord will testify of His Coming. Consider the following statements Jesus made at his first coming.

In the same context Jesus tells His disciples they will "know:"
* "so, you too, when you see all these things, recognize (know) that He is near, *right* at the door." **Matthew 24:33**

Jesus rebukes those who did not discern the times:
* "And in the morning, 'There will be a storm today, for the sky is red and threatening.' Do you know how to discern the appearance of the sky, but cannot discern the signs of the times?" **Matthew 16:3**

Noah knew when the wrath of the Lord was coming, but many did not:
* "For the coming of the Son of Man will be just like the days of Noah. For as in those days before the flood they were eating and drinking, marrying and giving in marriage, until the day that Noah entered the ark, and they did not understand until the flood came and took them all away; so will the coming of the Son of Man be." **Matthew 24:37-39**

John the Baptist's discernment of the times:
* "He said, 'I am A VOICE OF ONE CRYING IN THE WILDERNESS, "MAKE STRAIGHT THE WAY OF THE LORD,"' as Isaiah the prophet said.'" **John 1:23**

Simeon's awareness:
* "And there was a man in Jerusalem whose name was Simeon; and this man was righteous and devout, looking for the consolation of Israel; and the Holy Spirit was upon him. And it had been revealed to him by the Holy Spirit that he would not see death before he had seen the Lord's Christ." **Luke 2:25-26**

Awareness of the remnant:
* "At that very moment she came up and began giving thanks to God, and continued to speak of Him to all those who were looking for the redemption of Jerusalem." **Luke 2:38**

PRE-TRIBULATION RAPTURE ARGUMENTS

Who is the restrainer in 2 Thessalonians 2:6-7? "And you know what restrains him now, so that in his time he will be revealed. For the mystery of lawlessness is already at work; only he who now restrains *will do so* until he is taken out of the way."

The restrainer is a combination of two forces that currently restrain the Antichrist, referred to as something and someone by Paul in **2 Thessalonians 2:6-8**.
These forces will be removed to allow the Antichrist to come to a place of international political power.

Paul describes the restrainer of the Antichrist as a what (neuter in v. 6) and a He (masculine in v. 7).

Thus, the restraining force is a what and a He working together. Paul taught that the power of the state is appointed by God to restrain evil (**Rom. 13:1-4**). The power of the state is what, and the He is God and His sovereign decree. Some wrongly teach that the Holy Spirit is the restrainer who is removed when the Church is raptured before the Great Tribulation. If that were true, then nobody could be saved in the Great Tribulation, because it takes the work of the Holy Spirit moving on an unbeliever's heart in order for salvation to occur." - International House of Prayer

"Every person is to be in subjection to the governing authorities. For there is no authority except from God, and those which exist are established by God. Therefore whoever resists authority has opposed the ordinance of God; and they who have opposed will receive condemnation upon themselves. For rulers are not a cause of fear for good behavior, but for evil. Do you want to have no fear of authority? Do what is good and you will have praise from the same; for it is a minister of God to you for good. But if you do what is evil, be afraid; for it does not bear the sword for nothing; for it is a minister of God, an avenger who brings wrath on the one who practices evil." **Romans 13:1-4**

International House of Prayer, *100 Most Frequently Asked Questions About the End Times*, accessed through: http://www.mikebickle.org.edgesuite.net/MikeBickleVOD/2008/100_Most_Frequently_Asked_Questions_about_the_End_Times.pdf

PRE-TRIBULATION RAPTURE ARGUMENTS

Wasn't 70 AD the fulfillment of the destruction of the temple, and didn't Antiochus Epiphanes fulfill the 42 month tribulation in 171-165 BC?

What occurred in the past contained substantial partial fulfillments, but neither of these events has completely fulfilled the specific details of prophecy. Dual fulfillment prophecies are actually quite common in the scriptures.

Dual Fulfillment Prophecy:

• "For a child will be born to us, a son will be given to us; And the government will rest on His shoulders;" **Isaiah 9:6**

This scripture, within the same sentence, will be fulfilled in two different time periods. Yes, a Son (Jesus) has already been given and He has taken the keys to death, hell, and the grave: yet, the government will be fully on His shoulders when He returns during His second coming to reign here on earth and establishes His government.

• "But an hour is coming, and now is, when the true worshipers will worship the Father in spirit and truth; for such people the Father seeks to be His worshipers." **John 4:23**

Also, we must consider certain phrases given in the text and consider all tie ins:

We currently do not have everlasting righteousness in Jerusalem and all prophecy has not been fulfilled concerning the messiah.

• "Seventy weeks have been decreed for your people and your holy city, to finish the transgression, to make an end of sin, to make atonement for iniquity, to bring in everlasting righteousness, to seal up vision and prophecy and to anoint the most holy place." **Daniel 9:24**

Jesus' second coming has not taken place, nor has the end of the age. The age to come is when Jesus comes to reign physically here on earth. If this verse had already been fulfilled in its entirety, this would position the abomination of desolation at the end of the age and would also mean that we would have to look at all tie ins as occurring within the same timeframe.

- "As He was sitting on the Mount of Olives, the disciples came to Him privately, saying, "Tell us, when will these things happen, and what *will be* the sign of Your coming, and of the end of the age?..Therefore when you see the ABOMINATION OF DESOLATION which was spoken of through Daniel the prophet, standing in the holy place (let the reader understand)." **Matthew 24:3,15**

This tribulation period will exceed any trouble that has ever occurred on earth. The Holocaust was a more horrific time than what occurred in 70 AD or 171-165 BC. This would mean that the full fulfillment of these scriptures has not yet taken place.

- "For then shall be great tribulation, such as was not since the beginning of the world to this time, no, nor ever shall be." **Matthew 24:21**

Daniel's 70 Weeks
Daniel 9:24-27

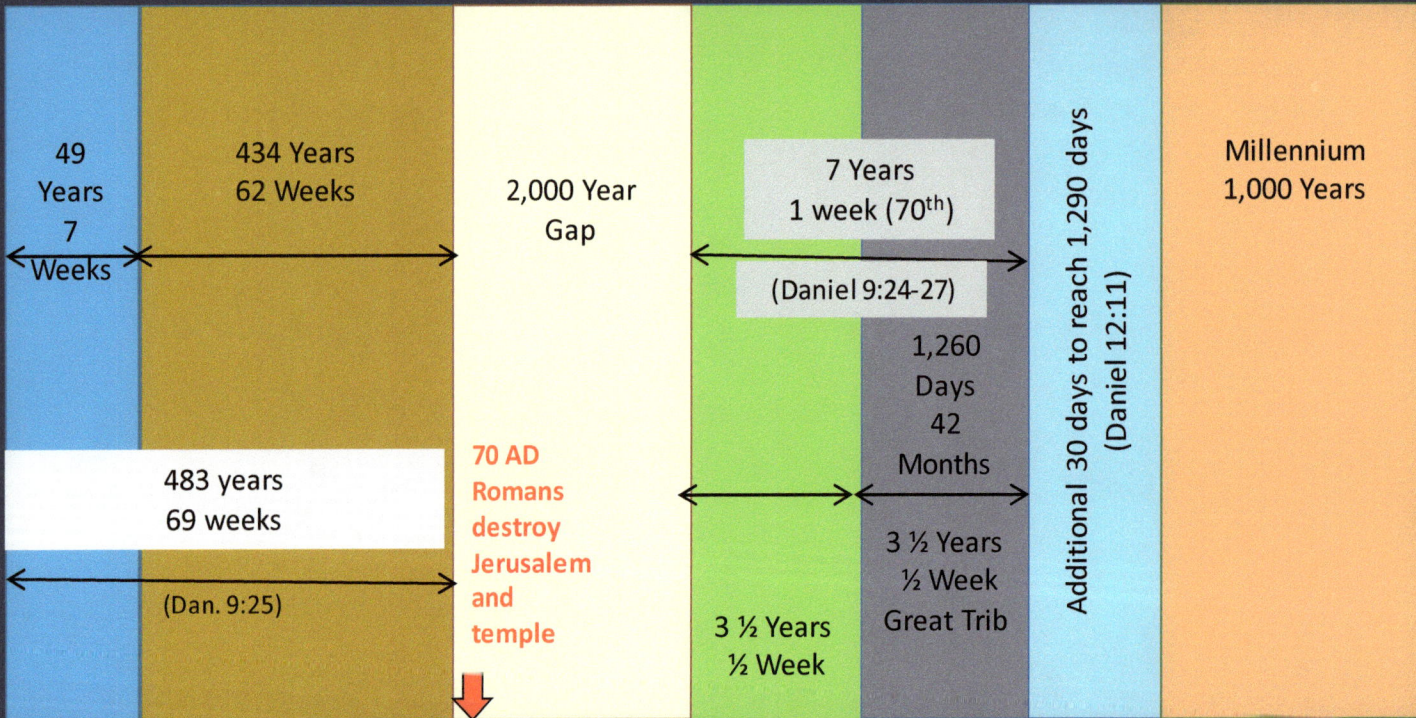

49 Years
7 Weeks

434 Years
62 Weeks

2,000 Year Gap

483 years
69 weeks

(Dan. 9:25)

70 AD Romans destroy Jerusalem and temple

7 Years
1 week (70th)

(Daniel 9:24-27)

3 ½ Years
½ Week

1,260 Days
42 Months

3 ½ Years
½ Week
Great Trib

Additional 30 days to reach 1,290 days
(Daniel 12:11)

Millennium
1,000 Years

"From the issuing of a decree to restore and rebuild Jerusalem…" **Daniel 9:25**

"…until the Messiah the Prince there will be seven weeks and sixty-two weeks…THEN after the sixty-two weeks the Messiah will be cut off and have nothing…" **Daniel 9:25-26**

"And he will make a firm covenant with the many for one week, but in the middle of the week he will put a stop to sacrifice and grain offering; and on the wing of abominations will come one who makes desolate, even complete destruction, one that is decreed, is poured out on the one who makes desolate." **Daniel 9:27**

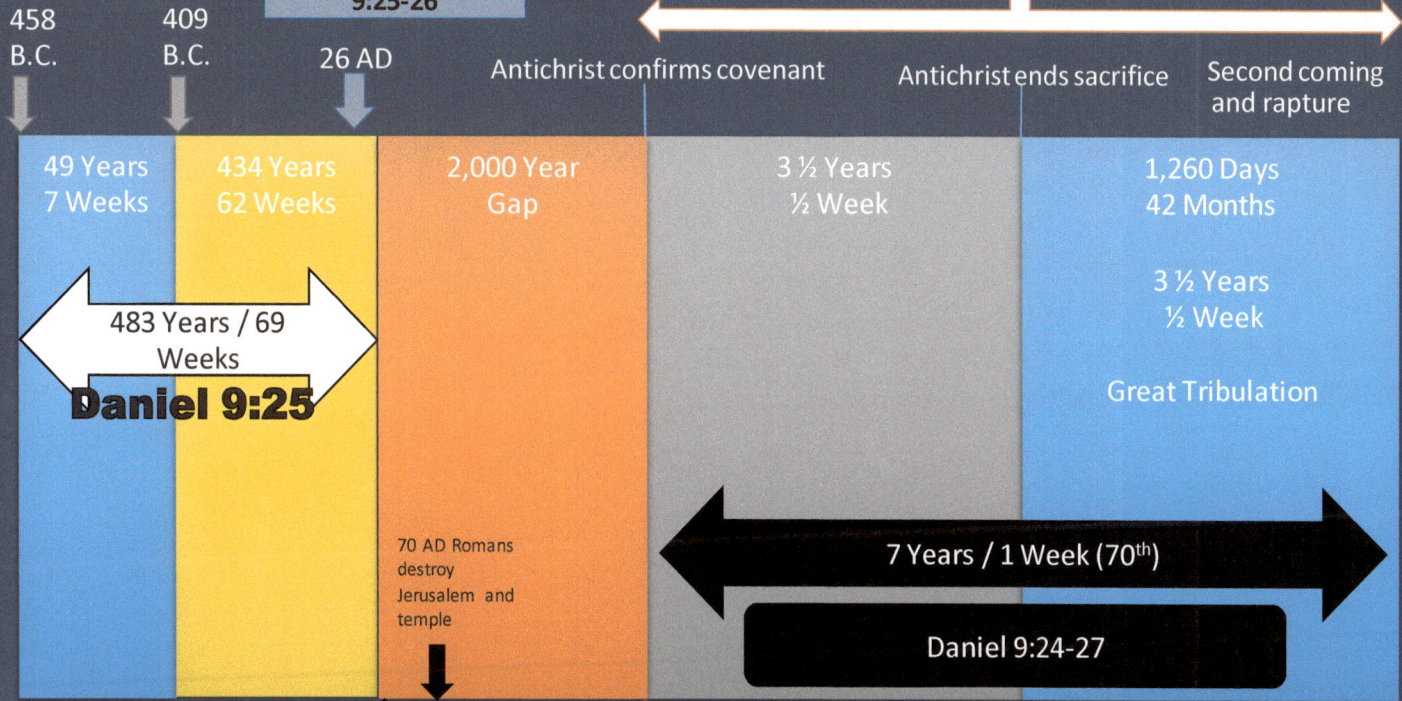

458 B.C.

409 B.C.

26 AD

Antichrist confirms covenant

Antichrist ends sacrifice

Second coming and rapture

49 Years 7 Weeks	434 Years 62 Weeks	2,000 Year Gap	3 ½ Years ½ Week	1,260 Days 42 Months 3 ½ Years ½ Week Great Tribulation

483 Years / 69 Weeks

Daniel 9:25

70 AD Romans destroy Jerusalem and temple

7 Years / 1 Week (70th)

Daniel 9:24-27

"Now this is the copy of the decree which King Artaxerxes gave to Ezra the priest, the scribe, learned in the words of the commandments of the Lord and His statutes for Israel" **Ezra 7:11**

"(Jesus' prophecy) not one stone will remain on top of another (destruction of temple)…" **Matthew 24:2**

"For you your selves know full well that the day of the Lord will come just like a thief in the night. While they are saying, "Peace and safety!" then destruction will come upon them suddenly like labor pains upon a woman with child, and they will not escape." **1 Thessalonians 5:2-3**

**Nebuchadnezzar's Dream
Daniel 2: The Statue**

HEAD OF GOLD
Babylon
626-539 BC

CHEST OF
SILVER
Medo-Persia
539-331 BC

THIGHS OF
BRONZE
Greece
331-146 BC

LEGS OF IRON AND
FEET OF IRON AND
CLAY
Roman and Antichrist
331-146 BC

**Daniel's Vision
Daniel 7: The Four Beasts**

LION
Babylon
626-539 BC

BEAR Medo-
Persia
539-331 BC

LEOPARD
Greece
331-146 BC

BEAST
With 10 horns
Antichrist's
empire

"And the dragon stood on the sand of the seashore.
Then I saw a beast coming up out of the sea, having ten horns and seven heads, and on his horns *were* ten diadems, and on his heads *were* blasphemous names. And the beast which I saw was like a leopard, and his feet were like *those* of a bear, and his mouth like the mouth of a lion. And the dragon gave him his power and his throne and great authority."
Revelation 13:1-2

The Composite Beast

"Then I desired to know the exact meaning of the fourth beast, which was different from all the others, exceedingly dreadful, with its teeth of iron and its claws of bronze, and which devoured, crushed and trampled down the remainder with its feet," **Daniel 7:19**

- "After this I kept looking in the night visions, and behold, a fourth beast, dreadful and terrifying and extremely strong; and it had large iron teeth. It devoured and crushed and trampled down the remainder with its feet; and it was different from all the beasts that were before it, and it had ten horns." **Daniel 7:7**
- "You, O king, were looking and behold, there was a single great statue; that statue, which was large and of extraordinary splendor, was standing in front of you, and its appearance was awesome." **Daniel 2:31**
- "Then another sign appeared in heaven: and behold, a great red dragon having seven heads and ten horns, and on his heads were seven diadems." **Revelation 12:3**
- "And the meaning of the ten horns that were on its head and the other horn which came up, and before which three of them fell, namely, that horn which had eyes and a mouth uttering great boasts and which was larger in appearance than its associates." **Daniel 7:20**
- "And the dragon stood on the sand of the seashore. Then I saw a beast coming up out of the sea, having ten horns and seven heads, and on his horns were ten diadems, and on his heads were blasphemous names." **Revelation 13:1**
- "The ten horns which you saw are ten kings who have not yet received a kingdom, but they receive authority as kings with the beast for one hour." **Revelation 17:12**
- "And the ten horns which you saw, and the beast, these will hate the harlot and will make her desolate and naked, and will eat her flesh and will burn her up with fire." **Revelation 17:16**
- "And I saw the beast and the kings of the earth and their armies assembled to make war against Him who sat on the horse and against His army." **Revelation 19:19**
- "The ten horns which you saw are ten kings who have not yet received a kingdom, but they receive authority as kings with the beast for one hour." **Revelation 17:12**

ANTICHRIST'S CHARACTERISTICS

DECEPTION AND CHARISMA:

❑ "King will arise, insolent (fierce) and skilled in intrigue (dark sayings)." **Daniel 8:23**

❑ "Through his shrewdness he will cause deceit to succeed by his influence." **Daniel 8:25**

❑ "By smooth words he will turn to godlessness those who act wickedly toward the covenant." **Daniel 11:32**

❑ "Such wisdom does not come down from heaven but is earthly, unspiritual, demonic." **James 3:15**

❑ "Great statue, extraordinary splendor, awesome appearance." **Daniel 2:31**

❑ "(LAST BEAST) different, EXCEEDINGLY DREADFUL." **Daniel 7:19**

❑ "White horse he who sat had bow…crown given to him…went conquering and to conquer." **Revelation 6:2**

❑ "Great dragon…called devil and Satan, who deceives whole world…gives power, throne, and great authority to beast." **Revelation 12:3-4, 9; 13:2**

❑ "Devil…murder from the beginning…no truth in him. Whenever he speaks a lie, he speaks from his own nature, for he is a liar and the father of lies." **John 8:44**

ANTICHRIST'S CHARACTERISTICS

DEMONIC DERIVED POWER:

- ❑ "Mighty but not by his own power." **Daniel 8:24**
- ❑ "On account of transgression the host will be given over to the horn along with the regular sacrifice." **Daniel 8:12**
- ❑ "Dragon gives power to the beast." **Revelation 13:2**
- ❑ "Fatal wound healed...whole earth amazed and followed after the beast...they worshiped dragon...and they worshiped the beast saying "who is like the beast, and who is able to wage war with him"...another beast like lamb and spoke like dragon...makes earth to worship first beast...cause as many as do not worship the beast to be killed." **Revelation 13:3-4, 11-12, 15**
- ❑ "You would have no authority over me, unless it had been given you from above." **John 19:11**

SUCCESS IN WILL: PERSECUTE ISRAEL, CHURCH, DEVOUR WHOLE EARTH:

- ❑ "Fourth beast (composite beast) will be different from all other kingdoms and will devour the whole earth and tread it down and crush it." **Daniel 7:23** (SEE ABOMINATION OF DESOLATION)
- ❑ "He will destroy to an extraordinary degree and prosper and perform his will; he will destroy mighty men and the holy people. And through shrewdness cause deceit to succeed by his influence." **Daniel 8:24-25**
- ❑ "The beast the comes out f abyss will make war with them, and overcome them and kill them (two witnesses)." **Revelation 11:7**
- ❑ "Then the dragon was enraged (because God keeps intervening for Israel)...and went to make war with those who keep God's commands and hold to the testimony of Jesus." **Revelation 12:17**

ANTICHRIST'S CHARACTERISTICS

<u>SUCCESS IN WILL: PERSECUTE ISRAEL, CHURCH, DEVOUR WHOLE EARTH:</u>

- ❑ "I kept looking, and that horn was waging war with the saints and overpowering them." **Daniel 7:21**
- ❑ "He will speak out against the Most High and wear down the saints of the Highest One, and he will intend to make alterations in times and in law; and <u>they will be given into his hand</u> for a time, times, and half a time." **Daniel 7:25**
- ❑ "<u>It was given to him</u> to make war with the saints and to overcome them, and authority over every tribe and people and tongue and nation <u>was given to him</u>." **Revelation 13:7**
- ❑ "White horse, and he who sat on it had a bow; and <u>a crown was given to him</u>, and he went out conquering and to conquer." **Revelation 6:2**
- ❑ "By smooth words he will turn to godlessness those who act wickedly toward the covenant, <u>BUT THE PEOPLE WHO KNOW THEIR GOD WILL DISPLAY GREAT STRENGTH AND TAKE ACTION.</u>" **Daniel 11:32**
- ❑ "And they overcame him because of the blood of the Lamb and the word of their testimony, and they did not love their life even when faced with death." **Revelation 12:11**
- ❑ "I kept looking, and that horn was waging war with the saints and overpowering them <u>UNTIL the ANCIENT OF DAYS came and judgment was passed in favor of the saints of the Highest One, and the time arrived when the saints took possession of the kingdom.</u>" **Daniel 7:21-22**

The Perfect End Time Plan is written in support of the end-time perspective of the early church (Historical Premillennialism), including those who were closest to the Apostles. It was written to give readers an overview of some of the main end-time themes prevalent in scripture. Most Christian's end-time views are based on inherited beliefs rather than personal convictions.

As I began to inquire about beliefs within my own stream of believers regarding our end time stance, there were not many answers. If I did receive an answer, it did not adequately address the sincere questions I had within my own heart, and many times, created more confusion. A couple of my main concerns with answers I received were consistency and vagueness.

As we begin to search out truth we must consider "the whole counsel of God." I have found that the views of the early church are the most consistent with scripture as a whole and this book clearly expresses those views. As you study this book along with scripture, I pray that the Holy Spirit will give you your own personal conviction.

This view is not widely publicized for a number of reasons including our tendency to shy away from any mention of suffering within the church. Secondly, many see the message of the judgment of the Lord as contradicting the message of the Love of Jesus. Yet, the zeal of God's justice and His love for man are two sides of the same coin. It is both the "goodness and severity of God." He is the "Lion" and the "Lamb."

God is first and foremost for His glory, and with His glory comes great responsibility. God disclosing Himself is His means of saving a lost world, and is the only answer for a generation who has embraced a perverted idea of love; having a definition of love as something that makes you feel good or happy, or the like. We must look to God's living word to find the purest, untainted definition of love. Love might effect our emotions, but love is an action. And in His perfect love Jesus is coming to act in love, to remove everything that hinders love.

What side will we find ourselves on when Jesus comes in His glory to give to everyone their just reward? There is no middle ground, and as there is a discernable escalation of God showing Himself, whatever is in our heart will surface like gold refined in the fire. Will we be offended when Jesus expresses Himself? Let us "Do homage to the Son, that He not become angry." May this book be a blessing to your life. "The Revelation of Jesus Christ" Revelation 1:1.

JOSHUA ALVAREZ (B. S. Southwestern Assembly of God University) is associate pastor at Unshackled Church in Pasadena, TX and author of *Navigating Through Grace*.

Contact: Joshuaalvarezbook@gmail.com